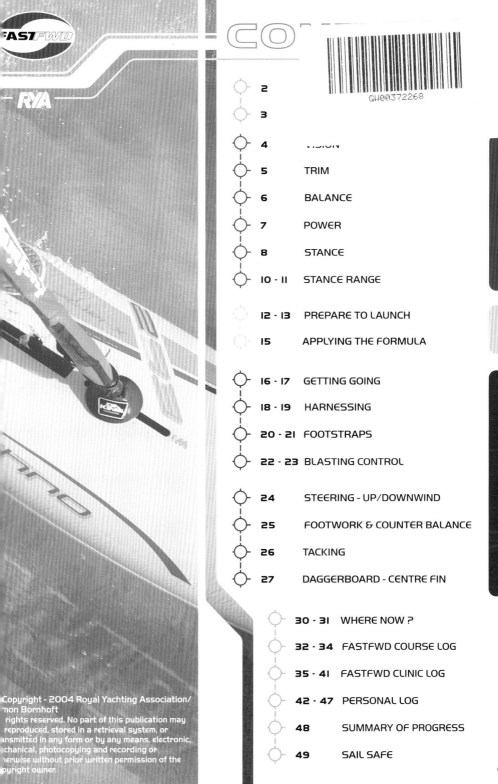

CO

GW00372268

FAST*FWD*

RYA

WELCOME TO Fastfwd

RYA Windsurfing
and Simon Bornhoft have
teamed up to create the new
RYA Windsurfing Scheme
'Fastfwd'.

Fastfwd is a dynamic, memorable
and incredibly effective coaching
system that offers remarkable
improvement for every level of
windsurfer. Fastfwd's logical and
proven methodology focuses
perfectly on what truly works on
the water for you. We really believe
Fastfwd will dramatically enhance
your windsurfing forever.

Fastfwd identifies, simplifies and
then fully embraces the most
influential skills in windsurfing.
It then encapsulates these skills in
a unique Formula, which is used
to experience and master all
aspects of the sport.

Fastfwd and its Formula not only
improve your current level, but
also form the backbone of your
future progression, by offering the
clearest and most instructive
guidance right through your
windsurfing career.

"We really look forward to
you becoming fluent in
Fastfwd"

VISION

STANCE

TRIM

FAST FWD

POWER

BALANCE

FAST FWD THE FORMULA

RYA — Vision helps maintain our sailing line.

- Vision relates to where we look and our angle to the wind.
- Vision helps us to judge situations and detect changes in sailing line.
- Vision hugely improves stability, stance and overall technique.
- Vision and using our head should be our first consideration.

Applying VISION

Look where you want to go!
Look forward for early planing, harnessing, footstraps and blasting control.
Look downwind to help turn downwind, increase speed or begin a gybe.
Look upwind to help turn upwind, control excess speed or start a tack.

FAST Notes

Vision sets your line and then enables you to adjust it to suit the conditions and the board's reactions. Start any fault diagnosis with Vision and don't underestimate the value of using your head! Avoid Gear Gazing. Looking down at the equipment is very destructive to your technique. For beachstarts, waterstarts and transitions, we recommend using specific Vision.

Trim keeps the board flat.

Trim is affected by where we stand and the forces directed through our feet.

Trim is influenced by all the other elements in the Formula.

Trim indicates if the rest of the Formula is working.

Trim is a priority for getting going, harnessing, footstraps and blasting control.

Applying TRIM

TRIM OUT OF FOOTSTRAPS
Front foot points forward to drive the board flat and forward.
Rear foot goes across the board to control sideways tilt.
Slower speeds - feet move forward and inboard, with increased toe pressure.
At higher speeds - feet move back and outboard, with increased heel pressure.

TRIM IN FOOTSTRAPS
To increase acceleration, apply pressure through toes.
To control acceleration, dig and weight heels and pull up on toes to lock windward rail down.

FAST Notes

Bending the back leg has a huge effect on **Trim**. Flexing the back leg takes weight off the tail when getting going and absorbs chop at speed. Specific tilt is used to steer or turn. e.g. tacking, heading upwind or gybing.

BALANCE

Balance forms our framework.

- **B** Balance maintains our distance from the rig by extending the front arm.

- **B** Balance means opposing the rig's position, forces and movement.

- **B** Balance contributes greatly to good Trim, Power and Stance.

- **B** Balance is a constant aim and the framework for good technique.

Applying BALANCE

RULE 1 : Maintain a good distance from the rig by extending your front arm.
Re-establish and exaggerate Balance to accelerate after getting into the harness and footstraps.

RULE 2: Always oppose the rig's position, force and movement to create a counter Balance.
Rig is leant back, the body leans or moves forward to counter Balance.
Rig is leant forward, the body leans or moves back to counter Balance.
Rig moves across the board, the body opposes the rig's movement to counter Balance.

FAST Notes

Neglect **Balance** by getting too close to, or moving in the same direction as the rig, and problems soon occur. Sometimes you may temporarily relax RULE 1 of Balance, (e.g. hooking-in, sailing very powered up, or mid-manoeuvre) but you will want to re-establish it quickly.

RYA | **Power channels the rig's forces.** |

(P) Power is the crucial action of sheeting the boom IN, BACK and DOWN.

(P) Power creates more drive by sheeting the sail IN and BACK.

(P) Power puts force DOWN through the mast base to improve Trim.

(P) Power is used constantly for getting going, harnessing, footstraps and blasting control.

Applying POWER

Power is best achieved when Balance is maintained with an extended front arm.
Power is applied out of the harness with the rear arm and shoulder.
Power is accentuated in the harness by sinking into correctly positioned harness lines.
In non-planing situations you limit Power.
In planing situations you often accentuate Power to control acceleration.

FAST Notes

In non-blasting situations, like beach/waterstarts or gybing, where the rig is not fully sheeted in, you still use the DOWN aspect of **Power** to increase your control over the rig and **Trim** the board. A high enough boom is needed to apply **Power** properly.
(See pages 12 and 13 Prepare to Launch)

RYA

Stance is how we use our body.

- ⓢ Stance relates to the alignment of our head, hips and heels.
- ⓢ Stance creates a range of movement and some very specific forces.
- ⓢ Stance is not about fixed positions.
- ⓢ Stance brings the whole Formula together.

Applying STANCE

The first four elements of the Formula establish the foundations of a Standard 7 Stance which can be used in and out of the harness.
VISION - Looking forward.
TRIM - Extended front leg, slightly bent back leg, feet shoulder width apart.
BALANCE - Extended front arm.
POWER - With the hands shoulder width apart the rear arm sheets in using body weight.

FAST Notes

Fastfwd uses a full Stance range, so like switching gear on a bike, you alter your body's alignment and forces to adapt to the rig's pull, the board's Trim and changing conditions. From your Standard 7 Stance, either 'lift and lock' towards a Straight 7, or 'drop and dig' towards a Super 7. (See pages 10 and 11 Stance Range)

simon BORNHOFT

○ 'Lift and Lock' towards a Straight 7 to increase speed and accelerate after getting into harness and footstraps. Often used as a light wind stance and for sailing through lulls.

○ STRAIGHT 7
- Narrow foot and hand spread to inside shoulder width.
- Extend the head and shoulders outboard to improve Balance.
- 'Lift and Lock' the hips, tightening the torso for extra effect.

○ STRAIGHT ▶

○ STANDARD ▶

○ SUPER ▶

STRAIGHT 7

○ 'Lift and Lock' the hips, extend the body and weight toes for full effect.

CONTROLLING ACCELERATION
'Drop and Dig'

RYA

'Drop and Dig' towards a Super 7 to control excess speed, for harnessing and locating footstraps at speed. Also used to cope with gusts and often as a strong wind stance.

SUPER 7
- Widen foot and hand spread to just past shoulder width.
- Drop hips down by bending the back leg.
- Dig heels to hold windward rail down (Pull up on the toes in the straps).
- Roll upper body slightly to accentuate the 'drop and dig' action.

SUPER 7

'Drop and Dig' to sink the hips and pull up on toes for full effect.

CHECK CHECK CHECK

RYA

◇ ▸**CHECK** THE CONDITIONS ▸**CHECK** YOUR EQUIPMENT ▸**CHECK** YOURSE

IT IS IMPERATIVE TO CHECK AND TUNE EQUIPMENT PRIOR TO EACH SAILING SESSION
DO NOT SAIL IN OFFSHORE WINDS, ALONE, OR IN CONDITIONS YOU ARE UNSURE OF.

CHECK ▸ MAST BASE/UJ AND EXTENSION ARE SECURE ▸ FIN BOLT IS FASTENED TIGHT
▸BOOM CLAMP IS SECURE ONTO MAST ▸OUTHAUL AND DOWNHAUL LINES ARE SECURE
AND NOT DAMAGED ▸UPHAUL IS ATTACHED SECURELY ▸HARNESS AND LINES ARE
FITTED CORRECTLY ▼

◇ SELECT RELEVANT SIZED BOARD AND RIG FOR CONDITIONS AND FINE TUNE ▼

I Boom Height

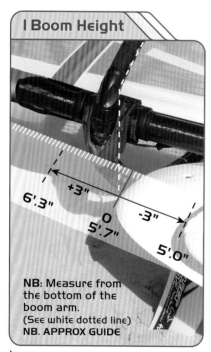

+3"
6'.3"
0
5'.7"
-3"
5'.0"

NB: Measure from
the bottom of the
boom arm.
(See white dotted line)
NB. APPROX GUIDE

▸ Check boom height in relation
to tail of board.

0 = 5'7"
Move +I"to 3" If between 5'7" ▸6'3"
Move –I"to 3" If between 5'7" ▸5'0"

2 Outhaul/Downhaul

▸ Tune downhaul and outhaul settings.

3 Harness Fixings

▸ Harness lines should be approximately a
hand's width apart.

RYA

4 Mast Base

Boards above 110L -
range 130 -145cm. Average
mast base position - 135cm
from the centre of mast base
to tail of board.

Boards below 110L -
range 125 -135cm. Average
mast base position - 130cm
from the centre of mast base
to tail of board.

5 Harness

▶ Make sure harness is
fitted tight.

6 Harness Line Length

▶ **Harness line length -**
Elbow to watchstrap for shortest length.
Elbow to end of palm for longest length.

7 Fin Sizes

▶ **Fin size formula for planing**

For boards above 110L: Sail size x 5 + 4 = Average
fin size in cm's. (E.g. 6m x 5 + 4 = 34cm.)

For boards below 110L: Sail size x 5 + 2 = Average
fin size in cm's. Your average fin size will probably
be suitable for most situations.

Tune down in size 1 - 4cm: Sailing well powered
up, lightweight and proficient sailors.

Tune up in size 1 - 4cm: Non planing, difficulty
sailing upwind or a heavyweight. For non-
planing/very marginal winds use 110L plus
formula and add up to 10cm, rather than 4cm.

RYA

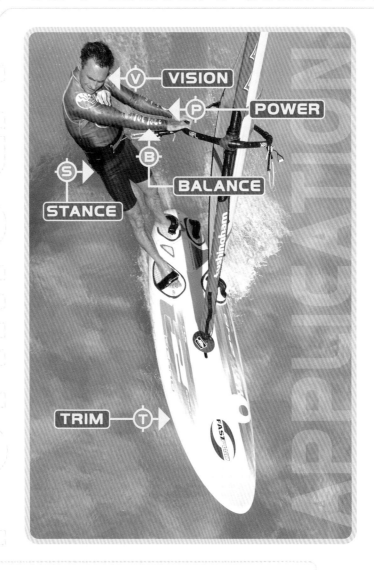

Labels on image: VISION, POWER, BALANCE, STANCE, TRIM

Ⓥ **VISION** helps maintain our sailing line

Ⓣ **TRIM** keeps the board flat

Ⓑ **BALANCE** forms our framework

Ⓟ **POWER** channels the rig's forces

Ⓢ **STANCE** is how we use our body

RYA

Getting going requires a specific process that's adapted to suit lighter or stronger winds.

(F) USING THE FORMULA TO GET GOING

(V) **VISION** Look forward to maintain a sailing line across the wind.
In marginal planing conditions **look and head downwind 5-15 degrees to promote early planing.**
In stronger winds **look and head upwind 5-15 degrees to dramatically improve control and hooking in.**

(T) **TRIM** Always force the board flat!
In light winds **both feet well forward and push through toes.**
In stronger winds **both feet further back, but still push through toes.**

(B) **BALANCE** Fully extend front arm and r᷂ forward to assist Trim and Power.
Body leans back to counter Balance and drive the board forward.

(P) **POWER** Pull down on the boom and sheet in and back as the board accelerat᷂

(S) **STANCE** Adopt a low Super 7 Stance and drop and push through your extende᷂ front leg.

SUPER 7

DROP AND PUSH

DROP + PUSH

AS THE BOARD STARTS TO PLANE
In lighter winds **shift towards a Straight 7 to accelerate.**
In stronger winds **shift towards a Super 7 to control acceleration.**
Once going, run through the Formula to prepare for harness and footstraps.

FAST Notes

'Drop and Push' through the toes to get going because the board is NOT planing fast and therefore the windward rail doesn't need the heels to dig and hold the rail down.

FAST*FWD*

RYA

LIGHT WIND

STRONG WIND

SUPER 7-DOWNWIND

FEET FORWARD

SUPER 7-UPWIND

FEET BACK

RYA

> **Harnessing commits our body to the rig, maintains power and takes the strain off the arms.**

F— FORMULA CHECK FOR HARNESSING

V— VISION Look forward to maintain your sailing line across the wind. Head slightly upwind to control excess speed, avoid catapults and encourage harness lines to windward prior to hooking in.

T— TRIM Position feet to maintain good Trim.

B— BALANCE Extend the front arm.

P— POWER Emphasise Power to sheet in and bring the harness line to windward.

S— STANCE In lighter winds shift towards a Straight 7 before and after hooking in.

In stronger winds shift towards a Super 7 to emphasise Power and keep the harness line to windward before and after hooking i

> **⊙— When the rest of the formula is working, the action of hooking in is simple.** ▼

❶▶

❷▶

❸▶

❹▶

❺▶

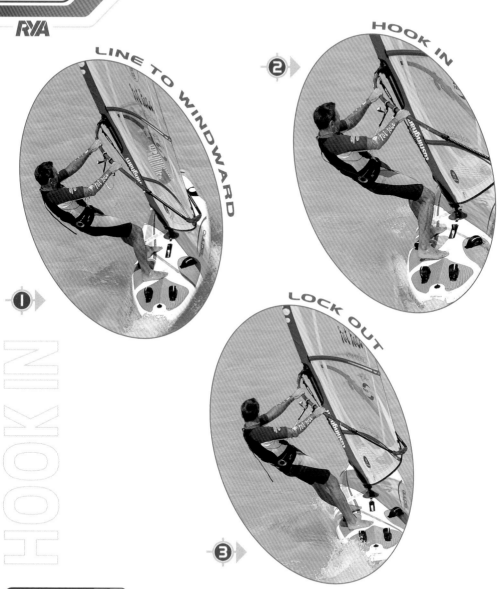

LINE TO WINDWARD

HOOK IN

LOCK OUT

HOOK IN

FAST Notes

To hook in, use a short, sharp pull on the boom to swing the line towards you, lifting your hips at the same time.

Whilst you might briefly glance at the line, re-establish **Vision** straight after.

Once hooked in, really commit your weight to the harness!

Run through the **Formula** to re-establish control and diagnose any problems.

Footstraps provide security and assist our ability to steer at speed.

(F) FORMULA CHECK FOR BOTH FOOTSTRAPS

(V) **VISION** Look forward to maintain your sailing line across the wind.

(T) **TRIM** Position moving foot next to strap.

(B) **BALANCE** Keep the front arm extended and counter Balance the body's movement with the rig.

(P) **POWER** Sink weight into harness and sheet-in to help Trim and un-weight feet.

(S) **STANCE** In light winds shift towards a 'Lift and Lock' Straight 7 before and after getting into footstraps.
In stronger winds shift towards a 'Drop and Dig' Super 7 before and after getting into footstraps.

(O) FRONT FOOTSTRAP ACTION 'Body Back – Rig Forward' ▼

(V) **VISION** Select the right sailing line to control board speed.

(T) **TRIM** Front foot just forward of the front strap. Light winds - back foot positioned behind front strap. Stronger winds - back foot positioned towards the back strap.

(B) **BALANCE** To unweight the front foot, sit back over a bent back leg, and at the same time move the rig forward to counter Balance.

Once in the front strap, swifty re-establish your Stance and run through the Formula. When settled run through back strap action

BODY BACK - RIG FORWARD as the front foot is slipped into the front strap.

⌖ BACK FOOTSTRAP ACTION 'Rig Back – Body Forward' ▼

ⓥ VISION Look and head upwind. Head further upwind to control excess speed.

ⓣ TRIM Place the back foot just forward of the back strap.

ⓑ BALANCE To unweight the back foot, rake the rig back and then lean the body forwards to counter Balance.

RIG BACK - BODY FORWARD as the back foot is slipped into the back strap.

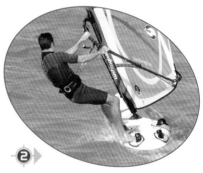

FAST Notes

Catapults and sudden luffing usually occur because **Vision** and sailing line were neglected and **Balance** and counter Balance deteriorated.

In super strong winds, it is possible to heavily sink the tail and get into the straps before the board actually planes. In this very specific case, the body sits back and the rig is held forward to **counter Balance**. Run through the Formula to maintain control and comfort and diagnose any problems.

For comfortable blasting always emphasise and develop good Vision, Trim, Balance, Power and Stance.

OUR '7' STANCE RANGE PLAYS A PIVOTAL ROLE WHEN ADAPTING TO CHANGES IN WIND, WATER STATE AND BOARD SPEED.

BLASTING CONTROL SCENARIOS

STRAIGHT 7

SCENARIO
Q: Losing speed?
A: Lift and Lock towards a really Straight 7 and bear away slightly.

STRAIGHT 7 (leaning forward)

SCENARIO
Q: Big Lull?
A: Body leans forward, often bending the front leg. The rig is kept sheeted in, but raked right back.

RYA

SUPER 7

SCENARIO
Q: Board bouncing around over the chop?
A: Drop and Dig towards an accentuated Super 7.

SUPER 7 (Accentuated)

SCENARIO
Q: Big Chop?
A: Accentuate your Super 7 and flex the back leg to absorb chop and prevent nose lift.

BLASTING CONTROL SITUATIONS

FAST Notes

Catapults often occur because of:
Poor **Vision**- Too far downwind when going for harness or footstraps.
Poor **Balance**- Body and rig lean forward at the same time.
Poor **Power**- Not enough Super 7 in the harness.

Stalling or Luffing often occurs because of:
Poor **Vision**- Looking down at the footstrap or harness line.
Poor **Trim**- Straight over-weighted back leg, or too much weight on the heels.
Poor **Balance**- Too close to boom or body and rig leaning towards the tail at the same time.

Steering is used to alter our sailing line and for the beginning or ending of transitions.

FORMULA FOR STEERING UPWIND

⬡ STEERING UPWIND

Altering course, preparing to get going in stronger winds, reducing blasting speed, sailing upwind or starting a tack.

VISION Look upwind.

TRIM Weight heels on windward rail.

BALANCE & POWER Extend front arm and rake the rig back.

STANCE SUPER 7 to initiate turn. STANDARD 7 and counter Balance as board heads up into wind.

NON-PLANING UPWIND

PLANING UPWIND

TRIM Curl toes and weight heels, especially the rear one. When planing upwind, it only takes subtle foot pressure to alter direction.

FORMULA FOR STEERING DOWNWIND

⬡ STEERING DOWNWIND

Altering course, encouraging planing, increasing planing speed, or entering a gybe

VISION Look downwind.

TRIM Extend front leg, pushing through toes.

BALANCE Extend front arm to angle mast forward.

POWER Sheet in to 'twist' the rig forward

STANCE SUPER 7 with hips down and back to counter Balance.

NON-PLANING DOWNWIND

PLANING DOWNWIND

TRIM Push through toes and ease back foot pressure. When planing it only takes subtle foot pressure to steer downwind.
STANCE Straight 7 in controllable winds.
Super 7 – Drop and Push in strong winds.

RYA

Footwork is a simple 3-step movement that allows us to Shift our weight and Switch our feet during the crucial part of tacks.

◯ FOOTWORK 'SHIFTING AND SWITCHING' ▼

SHIFTING is the action of transferring weight from one foot to another.

SWITCHING is the action of moving your foot from one position to another.

MID TACK - we 'Shift and Switch' when we move around the mast base.

❶ SHIFT

❷ SWITCH

❸ SHIFT

SHIFT
the hip over the front foot.

SWITCH
the back foot heel to toe.

SHIFT
the rear hip and back foot down the board.

◯ COUNTER BALANCE ▼

MID TACK
'Body Forward - Rig Back'

For transitions apply both rules of **Balance** to maintain a stable framework. However RULE 2 is heavily emphasised as the rig and body are constantly opposing each other's movement.

RULE 1 Maintain a good distance from the rig by extending the front arm.

RULE 2 Always oppose the rig's position, force and movement to create a **counter Balance**.

RYA

A tack can be used in both planing and non-planing conditions and works on high or low volume boards.

 FORMULA CHECK FOR TACKING

Tacking relies heavily on Vision, counter Balance and Footwork. Note how the beginning of the tack duplicates our upwind steering skills and the exit demonstrates our downwind steering skills.

ENTRY

VISION Look and sail upwind to start the tack.

COUNTER BALANCE Rig back, body forward, accentuate as board heads into wind.

FOOTWORK The front foot steps forward and wraps around the mast.

MID TACK

VISION Head turns to spot backhand gripping new side of boom.

COUNTER BALANCE Mast and body cross over, trying to maintain a good distance.

FOOTWORK As the Shift and Switch takes place, the head starts to spin round.

EXIT

VISION Head spins to look out of the tack

COUNTER BALANCE Rig is leant forward as body sinks back into a Super 7 on new tack.

FOOTWORK The new rear foot steps down the board to counter balance the forward rig.

FAST Notes

It is impossible to remember a whole sequence of instructions. So to improve your tacks, work through each element one at a time, starting with **Vision** then **counter Balance** and **Footwork**.

Ideally aim to sail without using a daggerboard or centre fin as this helps promote a more comfortable board when planing.

In ultra-light winds, or if you have to do a lot of upwind work, daggerboards and centre fins can provide more lateral resistance and ensure better upwind performance in non-planing situations.

VISION To help maintain your sailing line upwind really turn your shoulders and look into the wind.

DAGGERBOARD DOWN

TRIM With the daggerboard down you can tilt the board on the leeward rail when going upwind.

DAGGERBOARD UP

TRIM Going upwind without a daggerboard (or even with a small centre fin) the windward rail should always be depressed to provide grip.

FAST Notes

As you leave the shore, always head upwind before trying to get going. Equally, whenever you hit a lull, or stop planing, head into wind as you prepare for a new gust.

VISION

TRIM

STANCE

BALANCE

POWER

RYA

jon METCALFE

CARVE

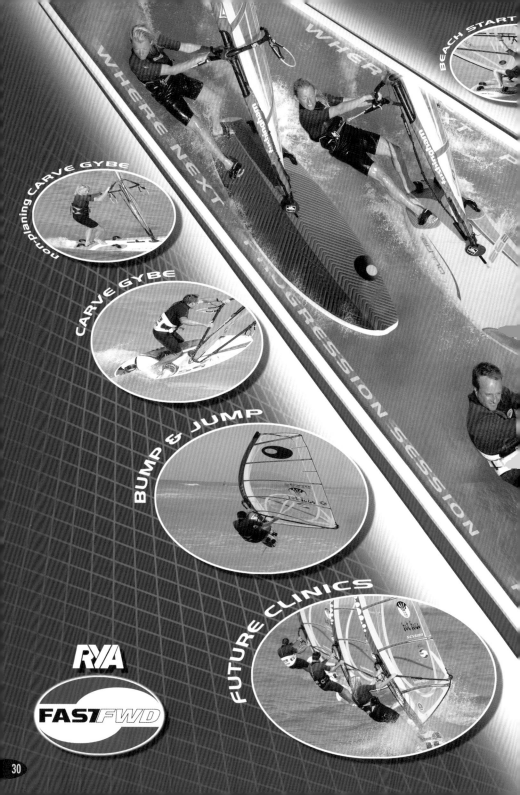

WHERE NEXT

BEACH START

non-planing CARVE GYBE

CARVE GYBE

BUMP & JUMP

PROGRESSION SESSION

FUTURE CLINICS

RYA

FAST FWD

30

WHERE NOW?

YOU HAVE JUST EXPERIENCED FASTFWD. SO WHAT'S NEXT?

The Formula is transferable into more dynamic aspects
of windsurfing! So let your aspirations and Fastfwd
guide your windsurfing future!

WATER START

FUN-FREE STYLE

FUTURE CLINICS

RYA

	COURSE DATA				
DATE	LOCATION	BOARD	RIG	WIND	CONDITIONS

COMMENTS ▶

FASTFWD FOCUS Ⓕ▶▶▶

	COURSE DATA				
DATE	LOCATION	BOARD	RIG	WIND	CONDITIONS

COMMENTS ▶

FASTFWD FOCUS Ⓕ▶▶▶

	COURSE DATA				
DATE	LOCATION	BOARD	RIG	WIND	CONDITIONS

COMMENTS ▶

FASTFWD FOCUS Ⓕ▶▶▶

RYA

| | | | | | COURSE DATA |
DATE	LOCATION	BOARD	RIG	WIND	CONDITIONS

COMMENTS ▶

FASTFWD FOCUS (F)▶▶▶

| | | | | | COURSE DATA |
DATE	LOCATION	BOARD	RIG	WIND	CONDITIONS

COMMENTS ▶

FASTFWD FOCUS (F)▶▶▶

| | | | | | COURSE DATA |
DATE	LOCATION	BOARD	RIG	WIND	CONDITIONS

COMMENTS ▶

FASTFWD FOCUS (F)▶▶▶

COURSE LOG

				COURSE DATA	
DATE	LOCATION	BOARD	RIG	WIND	CONDITIONS

COMMENTS ▶

FASTFWD FOCUS Ⓕ ▶▶▶

				COURSE DATA	
DATE	LOCATION	BOARD	RIG	WIND	CONDITIONS

COMMENTS ▶

FASTFWD FOCUS Ⓕ ▶▶▶

				COURSE DATA	
DATE	LOCATION	BOARD	RIG	WIND	CONDITIONS

COMMENTS ▶

FASTFWD FOCUS Ⓕ ▶▶▶

CLINIC LOG

CLINIC DATA

DATE	LOCATION	BOARD	RIG	WIND	CONDITIONS

CLINIC TYPE ▶

COMMENTS ▶

FASTFWD FOCUS ⒡ ▶▶▶

CLINIC DATA

DATE	LOCATION	BOARD	RIG	WIND	CONDITIONS

CLINIC TYPE ▶

COMMENTS ▶

FASTFWD FOCUS ⒡ ▶▶▶

CLINIC DATA

DATE	LOCATION	BOARD	RIG	WIND	CONDITIONS

CLINIC TYPE ▶

COMMENTS ▶

FASTFWD FOCUS ⒡ ▶▶▶

CLINIC DATA

DATE	LOCATION	BOARD	RIG	WIND	CONDITIONS

CLINIC TYPE ▶

COMMENTS ▶

FASTFWD FOCUS (F)▶▶▶

CLINIC DATA

DATE	LOCATION	BOARD	RIG	WIND	CONDITIONS

CLINIC TYPE ▶

COMMENTS ▶

FASTFWD FOCUS (F)▶▶▶

CLINIC DATA

DATE	LOCATION	BOARD	RIG	WIND	CONDITIONS

CLINIC TYPE ▶

COMMENTS ▶

FASTFWD FOCUS (F)▶▶▶

					CLINIC DATA
DATE	**LOCATION**	**BOARD**	**RIG**	**WIND**	**CONDITIONS**

CLINIC TYPE ▶

COMMENTS ▶

FASTFWD FOCUS Ⓕ ▶▶▶

					CLINIC DATA
DATE	**LOCATION**	**BOARD**	**RIG**	**WIND**	**CONDITIONS**

CLINIC TYPE ▶

COMMENTS ▶

FASTFWD FOCUS Ⓕ ▶▶▶

					CLINIC DATA
DATE	**LOCATION**	**BOARD**	**RIG**	**WIND**	**CONDITIONS**

CLINIC TYPE ▶

COMMENTS ▶

FASTFWD FOCUS Ⓕ ▶▶▶

RYA

CLINIC DATA

DATE	LOCATION	BOARD	RIG	WIND	CONDITIONS

CLINIC TYPE ▶

COMMENTS ▶

FASTFWD FOCUS Ⓕ ▶▶▶

CLINIC DATA

DATE	LOCATION	BOARD	RIG	WIND	CONDITIONS

CLINIC TYPE ▶

COMMENTS ▶

FASTFWD FOCUS Ⓕ ▶▶▶

CLINIC DATA

DATE	LOCATION	BOARD	RIG	WIND	CONDITIONS

CLINIC TYPE ▶

COMMENTS ▶

FASTFWD FOCUS Ⓕ ▶▶▶

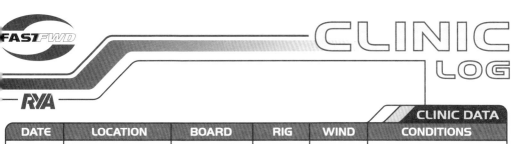

					CLINIC DATA
DATE	LOCATION	BOARD	RIG	WIND	CONDITIONS

CLINIC TYPE ▶

COMMENTS ▶

FASTFWD FOCUS Ⓕ ▶▶▶

					CLINIC DATA
DATE	LOCATION	BOARD	RIG	WIND	CONDITIONS

CLINIC TYPE ▶

COMMENTS ▶

FASTFWD FOCUS Ⓕ ▶▶▶

					CLINIC DATA
DATE	LOCATION	BOARD	RIG	WIND	CONDITIONS

CLINIC TYPE ▶

COMMENTS ▶

FASTFWD FOCUS Ⓕ ▶▶▶

RYA

CLINIC DATA

DATE	LOCATION	BOARD	RIG	WIND	CONDITIONS

CLINIC TYPE ▶

COMMENTS ▶

FASTFWD FOCUS Ⓕ▶▶▶

CLINIC DATA

DATE	LOCATION	BOARD	RIG	WIND	CONDITIONS

CLINIC TYPE ▶

COMMENTS ▶

FASTFWD FOCUS Ⓕ▶▶▶

CLINIC DATA

DATE	LOCATION	BOARD	RIG	WIND	CONDITIONS

CLINIC TYPE ▶

COMMENTS ▶

FASTFWD FOCUS Ⓕ▶▶▶

RYA

CLINIC DATA

DATE	LOCATION	BOARD	RIG	WIND	CONDITIONS

CLINIC TYPE ▶

COMMENTS ▶

FASTFWD FOCUS Ⓕ ▶ ▶ ▶

CLINIC DATA

DATE	LOCATION	BOARD	RIG	WIND	CONDITIONS

CLINIC TYPE ▶

COMMENTS ▶

FASTFWD FOCUS Ⓕ ▶ ▶ ▶

CLINIC DATA

DATE	LOCATION	BOARD	RIG	WIND	CONDITIONS

CLINIC TYPE ▶

COMMENTS ▶

FASTFWD FOCUS Ⓕ ▶ ▶ ▶

RYA

DATE	LOCATION	BOARD	RIG	WIND	SAILING DATA CONDITIONS

DATE	LOCATION	BOARD	RIG	WIND	SAILING DATA CONDITIONS

DATE	LOCATION	BOARD	RIG	WIND	SAILING DATA CONDITIONS

LOG

RYA

					SAILING DATA
DATE	LOCATION	BOARD	RIG	WIND	CONDITIONS

					SAILING DATA
DATE	LOCATION	BOARD	RIG	WIND	CONDITIONS

					SAILING DATA
DATE	LOCATION	BOARD	RIG	WIND	CONDITIONS

DATE	LOCATION	BOARD	RIG	WIND	SAILING DATA CONDITIONS

DATE	LOCATION	BOARD	RIG	WIND	SAILING DATA CONDITIONS

DATE	LOCATION	BOARD	RIG	WIND	SAILING DATA CONDITIONS

RYA

					SAILING DATA
DATE	LOCATION	BOARD	RIG	WIND	CONDITIONS

					SAILING DATA
DATE	LOCATION	BOARD	RIG	WIND	CONDITIONS

					SAILING DATA
DATE	LOCATION	BOARD	RIG	WIND	CONDITIONS

RYA

					SAILING DATA	
DATE	LOCATION	BOARD	RIG	WIND	CONDITIONS	

					SAILING DATA	
DATE	LOCATION	BOARD	RIG	WIND	CONDITIONS	

					SAILING DATA	
DATE	LOCATION	BOARD	RIG	WIND	CONDITIONS	

PERSONAL LOG

SAILING DATA

DATE	LOCATION	BOARD	RIG	WIND	CONDITIONS

SAILING DATA

DATE	LOCATION	BOARD	RIG	WIND	CONDITIONS

SAILING DATA

DATE	LOCATION	BOARD	RIG	WIND	CONDITIONS

SUMMARY OF PROGRESS

NAME

TEL

EMAIL

FASTFWD INTRO

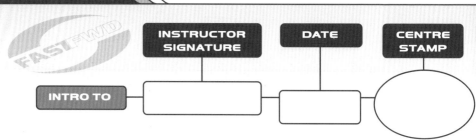

| INTRO TO | INSTRUCTOR SIGNATURE | DATE | CENTRE STAMP |

Completion confirms that the owner of this logbook has been introduced to the Fastfwd Formula and its principles.

FASTFWD COMPETENCE

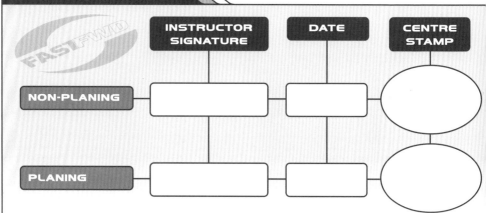

	INSTRUCTOR SIGNATURE	DATE	CENTRE STAMP
NON-PLANING			
PLANING			

Completion confirms that the owner of this logbook has demonstrated a level of competence by:

• correctly choosing and setting up a board and rig suitable for his/her size and the prevailing conditions.

• launching and recovering this equipment.

• demonstrating an understanding of, and being able to apply, all relevant areas of Fastfwd.

• maintaining his/her sailing position in relation to the wind, sailing both close to and away from the wind, showing a full stance range, and returning to his/her starting point on the shore, tacking efficiently and steering to avoid collision.

• demonstrating an ability to sail safely and in control, and an awareness of the dangers of his/her environment.

• taking the necessary actions to prevent the need to be rescued and knowing how to summon or give assistance if required.